# Called 2 Care
*The biblical case for Care Groups...*

by
**Dan Vis**

All Scripture quotations are from the
King James Version of the Bible
Emphasis supplied unless otherwise indicated.

ISBN: 978-1-958155-12-7

Published by FAST Missions
111 2nd Street
Kathryn, ND 58049

Additional copies of this book are available by
visiting us at WWW.FAST.ST

# Dedication

*This book is dedicated to Johnny & Tina, and the amazing group at Gateway who have demonstrated unequivocally the power of Care Groups to change lives, win souls, and plant churches...*

# Table of Contents

# Crash Course
## Preface

As you'll discover in the first chapter, I've been on a quest, nearly my whole adult life. Inspired by the potential of spiritual multiplication, I've been searching for a model of evangelism by which the average person can become an effective soul-winner.

I didn't expect that quest to take so long, or to be so difficult. But it has. In fact, I began to wonder if my quest might be in vain.

Ultimately, it wasn't until I had visited scores, maybe even hundreds of churches--that I finally found what I was looking for. It was a fresh church plant in downtown Melbourne, Australia--one of the most secular cities in the world. It was a thriving church, filled with happy committed believers. Most of them had been recently won to Christ by a friends. Most of them were now busy working to win others. I had never seen anything like it.

This book is a brief study into the biblical foundation of small groups. Or more specifically, a certain kind of small group--called a Care Group. You'll discover the secrets to building a thriving Care Group ministry in your church, and some of the obstacles likely to get in your way. If you're ready to see your church transformed, or just eager to start winning souls yourself, this book can help.

I've been back to Gateway multiple times in the years since, and kept in touch with several friends there. They've stayed the course. Gateway has now grown to four congregations, and alumni are planting even more churches around the world.

There's no question Care Groups can work. This book is sent out with a prayer it can help Care Groups work for you...

# The Long Quest
## Chapter 1

Have you ever found yourself studying the book of Acts, and wondering how they did it? You read of their amazing evangelistic successes, and it's easy to feel discouraged. Maybe even overwhelmed. Why don't we see these kinds of things happening today? Is there some key they knew, that we've forgotten. Some long lost engine of evangelism?

I believe there is, and in this course I want to make a case for what I see as that forgotten key. That missing engine of evangelism. And fortunately, it is something that could be dusted off and recovered today, and would give evangelistic success in our day too.

In fact, I've seen it with my own eyes. But let me start by telling a bit of my story...

### Early Experiences

I stumbled my way into Christianity as a young man, just barely into my twenties. I didn't have any real religious background, and started out with a lot of confused ideas. But I had the good fortune to have a few good friends who took me under their wing and helped me get started in the Christian life. They taught me how to study, pray, deal with temptation, share my faith and more.

One of the thing they shared especially resonated with me: a vision for spiritual multiplication. The potential of one average Christian if they could just learn to reproduce consistently. By merely winning one friend a year, to Christ, and then teaching them to do the same—that one person could multiply to a thousand in ten years, a million in twenty, and a billion in just ten years more. The numbers were absolutely compelling.

But there was a catch. It required the ability to teach the average person to win souls—consistently. If that could not be achieved, the whole chain reaction would fail.

So I set out to try and learn that skill. And I had some measure of success. I spent a whole summer knocking on doors, sharing the Gospel. I tried my hand at public evangelism, on multiple occasions. I learned how to give Bible studies and began studying with people. And while I grew through all these experiences, and had some amazing encounters—and even saw a few baptisms—I never quite felt like I had something that would work consistently. And certainly not something I could pass on to another person easily.

My dream of multiplication began to feel jeopardized.

One day I went up to my pastor and asked him a question. Basically, did he know any lay person in the state where I lived, that was regularly winning souls to Christ. That is, consistently, year in, year out. If there was, I figured I might be able to visit them, and learn their method. But he scratched his head for a moment, and then slowly said no. He didn't know a single person anywhere that was doing that.

That got me thinking there had to be a problem with how our churches were training our members. And it started me down a quest, to find a church that was doing it right. Someone, somewhere, that was equipping people for effective ministry—in a way that enabled the average person to begin winning their friends to Christ. Spiritual multiplication could not happen any other way.

That ended up being a rather long, and difficult quest.

Moving forward, I continued to be involved in full-time ministry, serving God as a teacher, speaker, administrator, writer, and pastor. And over the course of time probably visited hundreds of congregations. Everywhere, it seemed, churches were facing the exact same problem. Multiplication wasn't happening anywhere. Why? Because the average member was not being equipped to win souls.

## An Answer at Last

To make a long story short, I ended up visiting a new church plant in Melbourne, Australia one year, called Gateway. They had heard about my work in discipleship, and had invited me to come over and do some training for their members. It was my first time to travel down under, and I was excited about the opportunity to visit. Little did I know my life was about to be changed forever.

As excited as I was to share what I know about living the Christian life, I was even more excited by what I saw. It was a young church, filled with college students and young professionals. There was an energy and enthusiasm that was contagious—an excitement that was palpable. And as I began getting to know some of the people there, I was shocked to discover that most of them were relatively new Christians who had been led to Christ in that church. And even more surprising, many of them had already begun winning others to Christ as well. Everywhere, it seemed, the average member was just a few years old and had already brought someone else to faith. Some had second and third generation spiritual descendants!

For the first time in my life, I was seeing real live multiplication in action. And I was fascinated. Over the next decade, I made several more trips to Australia, to do training, but also to learn. And each year the story was even more impressive. Once their numbers grew, they planted a second church. Then a third. Then their daughter church planted another church. Soon there were multiple churches, each preparing new church plants of their own.

And at everyone one of these groups I saw the same thing: young people on fire for God—new to faith but already winning souls. It was astonishing, actually. New Testament like multiplication was taking place right before my eyes, and it was happening in one of the most secular, Gospel-hardened cities in the world. I was watching something I have never seen any church do better, before or since.

What was the secret to their evangelistic success? It was a simple idea really. Something I had never done much with: small groups. Or more specifically, Care Groups. They had developed a whole model for reaching out to friends by opening their homes and building real relationships. And wherever this model went, it was giving results.

During my many visits to Gateway, I studied carefully what they were doing. I asked lots of questions, talked to key people, participated in Care Group meetings first hand, and learned everything I could. And little by little, I began to understand how these groups worked, and why. I also began digging deep into the Scriptures, and was shocked to discover the same model they followed was there all along.

In the coming days we are going to dig deep into this Care Group model of ministry, exploring both its biblical roots, and its modern day application.

May it prove to be the answer to your quest too!

# The Long Quest
## Study Questions

Why is spiritual multiplication the only way to finish the work?

Explain what "the catch" is to making this work?

Why do you think most churches are having trouble training the average person to win souls?

Explain the method used by Gateway to win souls so consistently?

Additional Notes:

# The Right Foundation
## Chapter 2

Yesterday we looked at the power of spiritual multiplication, and its potential to finish the work. Personally, I'm convinced it is the only way the work can ever be finished. That's why I've given my life to disciple-making, to helping others grow in their walk with God.

But there's definitely a catch. For spiritual multiplication to work, there has to be a way to equip the average member to become a soul winner. And it took me a long while to find a church where that was actually happening. And they used a method I had never really considered: Care Groups.

Today, I want to take a little time to look at why this approach is such a powerful model for evangelism. But first, let's look at how we typically do evangelism today...

**Modern Approaches**

Churches today run all sorts of training programs, but few succeed at equipping believers to actually become effective, consistent soul winners. These programs may help members grow in specific areas of discipleship, like prayer, or Bible study, or they may help them do a better job at running some church program—but if these programs fail to equip the average

Christian to begin leading their friends and family to Christ, year in, year out, the Great Commission will never be fulfilled.

I believe the reason these programs aren't working, has to do with the methods we typically use to win souls. Consider the following:

*Public Evangelism*

In many churches, the emphasis is on public evangelism. While important, this approach has limitations. First, it is generally quite expensive, which makes it hard to do sustainably. And it can be exhausting for church members to come out night after night when they already have full time jobs and plenty of home responsibilities. It also tends to encourage members to think evangelism is a seasonal event rather than an ongoing lifestyle—something you do now and then at certain times of the year. It can also start to feel a bit like a spectator sport. It communicates the idea evangelism is something you come out and watch someone else do.

Worse, seekers who come to evangelistic meetings often have little or no connection to people inside the church. This makes it quite difficult to persuade them to respond to appeals to join a new church. And those who do, frequently drift away soon after the evangelist leaves, because they don't have any strong relationship ties to hold them. This is especially true, if there is no systematic follow-up plan in place.

But here's what makes this approach even more problematic, few members are going to feel comfortable doing this kind of evangelism. The thought of preaching before a crowd petrifies the average believer. And few are going to feel comfortable doing this. So without intending to, we give the impression evangelism is the work of professionals, that it's limited to a select few.

*Bible Work*

Other churches focus on urging members to go to the people in their neighborhoods and offer personal sit-down Bible studies in their homes. But this approach, while also important, has problems of its own. For many, knocking on doors can be just as scary as preaching, if not more! And sticking with this kind of work, week after week, when you are out there isolated and alone can be challenging. It's hard enough to get someone to start giving Bible studies, but harder still to get them to continue in that for any sustained length of time.

Furthermore, the Bible worker training we give is often quite superficial, giving only the briefest introduction to the questions a person will face in the field. And often, they are not even the right questions! Practically speaking, it's easy to teach the mechanics of how to do a study with someone, but there are an endless array of questions people are likely to face, and a solid preparation takes more training. Without that, many members will be reluctant to get involved, rightly sensing they are deficient in skills and knowledge, and unprepared for all those bewildering Bible questions they are sure to encounter.

And perhaps more significant, these same members may have gifts or strengths that would qualify them to witness effectively in other ways. Trying to squeeze every person into the exact same ministry mold, and especially when that mold doesn't really fit—only leaves people feeling frustrated and stifled. And ultimately they may end up concluding evangelism just isn't for them. So once again, we end up with only a small percentage of our members willing to engage in this kind of ministry.

Here's the bottom line: if our goal is more workers, we must find an engine for evangelism that will make it possible to mobilize every member possible. Neither of these are great candidates. There has to be some other way. Seriously: other than your pastor, what percentage of the members in your church do regular public evangelistic meetings, or give regular personal Bible studies?

## The Care Group Solution

As you can guess by now, I believe we've been building our evangelism on the wrong foundation. That the key to mobilizing a bigger percentage of our church members, is to follow a different approach. And in particular: evangelistic small groups, or more specifically, Care Groups.

Consider some of the advantages to this approach:

First and foremost, this is something any believer can get involved with, and even enjoy. Not every person feels ready to preach a sermon or give a Bible study, but they can all participate in a Care Group. Members with more teaching experience can lead out in the Bible study. Others can support the meetings by bringing a dish, or giving a ride to a guest. Friendly members can offer engaging conversation. Those with a suitable house, might open their home as a meeting location. Timid members can support the group just by showing up, and smiling. And everyone can invite a friend, and pray! The point is, every person can fit in somewhere, and serve where they fit best.

Better still, Care Groups solve virtually all the problems with our other more modern approaches. It is not expensive, nor exhausting. It doesn't produce spectators, and it's not seasonal. It builds strong relationships between believers and those seeking Christ, and it has built in follow-up and support for those who choose Christ. It is easier to get church members involved, and it is easier to maintain motivation. Group members can participate in ways appropriate to their skill and knowledge, and their responsibilities can expand naturally as they grow in experience. And commitment.

If you are looking for a way to mobilize the average member, and give them evangelistic success, this is it.

## The Right Foundation

This is not to say there is not a place for public evangelism, or personal Bible studies. There is. In fact, both are critically important. What I am suggesting is that running Care Groups proves a better foundation for evangelism. And that's because it's the only approach that will allow you to mobilize a bigger proportion of your church. It's a question of prioritization.

Actually, we've been told this is the foundation to prioritize. Consider these quotes from that tried and true book Christian Service:

> *In our churches let companies be formed for service. Let different ones unite in labor as fishers of men.*
>
> *If there is a large number in the church, let the members be formed into small companies.*
>
> *If in one place there are only two or three who know the truth, let them form themselves into a band of workers.*
>
> *The formation of small companies as a basis of Christian effort is a plan that has been presented before me by One who cannot err. Christian Service, p 72.*

Read that last quote again carefully. It's not only suggesting that small groups (or small companies) are a good way to do outreach, it's saying that this should be the basis (or foundation) of our efforts. Public evangelism, and personal

Bible work are important, but they work best when built on top of broad participation in Care Groups. To put it differently, I'm not saying we need less public evangelism, or less Bible work. In contrast, I believe we need more. But both of these will both work better when ample groundwork is being done through small groups.

Suppose you had a half dozen small groups going in your church, each one is growing steadily. They meet weekly, enjoying good food and fellowship. They study the Bible together, and pray for and with each other. And best of all, there are seekers in every group, growing in their relationship with God.

Now suppose you were a pastor. Would you be more or less inclined to do public evangelism? More of course, because you have a growing group of people likely to come out—and you don't even have to spend thousands of dollars to get them to come. These Care Groups just bring their friends.

And what about personal Bible studies? Do you think there would be more less going on in your church? More, because the seekers in these groups would be asking Bible questions. And the members in those groups would be happy to study with them and answer those questions. Why? Because they have become friends!

In other words, Care Groups are not a replacement for public evangelism or Bible work. Rather, they need to become a new foundation in our churches. One that is intentional about trying to mobilize every member possible for ministry involvement. And if we make that change, it will actually revitalize all the other ministries in our church. Particularly, public evangelism and Bible work.

This is what I saw in Gateway, that church I visited in Australia. Lots of public evangelism, and lots of Bible work. And these efforts were yielding strong results, primarily because the vast majority of their members were involved in Care

Groups. It didn't replace these other approaches, it energized them.

Care Groups can do the same in your church. But before getting to what it will take to make this transition, let's pause a moment and look at some of the biblical evidence for Care Groups...

# The Right Foundation
## Study Questions

Take a moment to list some of the limitations of public evangelism:

What are some of the obstacles to focusing largely on personal Bible work?

What are some of the advantages to using Care Groups as the foundation of your outreach efforts?

Why do you think it lacks the disadvantages of most other methods?




What plan are we counseled to use as "a basis of Christian effort"?




Explain how this approach strengths, rather than weakens, both public evangelism and personal Bible work.




Additional Notes:

# Clear Instructions
## Chapter 3

Jesus left clear instructions to His church: take the Gospel to the entire world. And the early church did just that. The Gospel went everywhere in just one generation. Christianity became the most extraordinary movement in history.

But I believe the reason for their success is actually quite simple: Jesus not only told them what to do, but how. And the early church simply followed His instructions. If we want to see similar results today, it makes sense to study the biblical record and see if we can't tease out some of that instruction. And then follow it once more.

### The Master Evangelist

Jesus of course, was the epicenter of this evangelistic explosion. And He gave His original instructions about how to do this work to His disciples. In his training of the twelve for example, He spent a whole chapter detailing exactly how to do ministry, and it revolved around this key point:

> *Matthew 10:11*
> *And into whatsoever city or town ye shall enter, enquire who in it is worthy; and there abide till ye go thence.*

In other words, find one key home and use that home as a base for ministry. Later, when giving similar instructions to the seventy, He repeated the same basic instruction—to go find one house "and in the same house remain". In fact, He even added "go not from house to house" (Luke 10:7). Their ministry was to be centered in homes.

And Jesus Himself, modeled this approach. While He clearly had a special calling as an itinerant preacher, we frequently find Him using homes for ministry. The New Testament reports Him using the homes of Peter, Matthew, Simon, Zacchaeus, and Lazarus. And there are references to homes He used in Capernaum, Jerusalem, and elsewhere. No doubt Jesus loved the personal interaction that is possible when you spend time with people in their homes.

Near the end of His ministry, He gave His disciples even more explicit instructions about what would be the key to their evangelistic success. In particular, He said that genuinely caring for fellow believers would be our source of power: "by this shall all men know that ye are my disciples, if ye have love one to another" (John 13:35). A few chapters later, He made it clear that unity would be another vital key. His apostolic prayer was that we all "may be one ... that the world may believe" (John 17:20-21). So if we are serious about wanting to reach all men, and see those in the world come to faith—these are twin keys we need to use.

Jesus is here explaining that our most compelling argument is not going to be a thick stack of proof texts—but rather, our ability to model true Christian community. That when people discover a group of believers who have kind, caring compassion for one another, and warm, genuine fellowship, they will be drawn to it like a moth to the flame. In a lost, lonely world, a Care Group is in fact, a miracle.

This is one reason, by the way, public evangelism and personal Bible work are so limited on their own. We may be impressed by an evangelist and find him engaging and charismatic. But we don't really have a chance to see how he engages with other believers when he is speaking from a stage. And similarly, while we may like the person giving us Bible studies, and find them friendly and nice, we don't really get a chance to see how they relate to fellow Christians. In both of these cases, we throw out the very things Jesus said would bring success: love for one another, and unity with each other. But when sitting around a living room with a core team of believers, seekers see exactly how we interact with each other. And genuine caring has a magnetic power.

## Pentecost

This same idea of using homes for work continued after Jesus ascended. On the day of Pentecost, approximately 3000 souls were baptized and the Christian church was born. This led the apostles to the difficult question of how to organize and nurture this flood of new believers. What approach did they take?

The book of Acts reveals that their solution was to organize them into small groups, meeting "from house to house" (Acts 2:46). We even have a good idea what these early gatherings were like:

*Acts 2:42*
*And they continued stedfastly in the apostles'*
*doctrine and fellowship, and in breaking of*
*bread, and in prayers.*

There was Bible study, personal sharing, prayer, and food! This is the exact pattern I found followed in the Care Groups I experienced in Australia. In fact, these groups were modeled on Acts 2 explicitly.

These early groups also fostered a powerful sense community. They generously and sacrificially met one another's needs (Acts 2:44-45). The people enjoyed a beautiful sense of unity, continuing "with one accord" (Acts 2:46). In fact, they demonstrated such "gladness and singleness of heart" that everyone around looked on with "favour" and the Lord was able to add "to the church daily such as should be saved" (Acts 2:47). The keys of love and unity were clearly working here!

And note that it wasn't just one or two houses. Later, we read that the Jerusalem church continued to "teach and preach Jesus Christ" "in every house" (Acts 5:42). If you were a believer it was just assumed you would open your house for evangelism. Granted, the apostles would sometimes go and preach at the temple, and I'm sure there were some personal Bible studies going on—but for the average member, evangelism took place primarily in homes.

**The Apostle Paul**

Paul seems to have embraced this model, and spread it throughout the ancient world. The Bible records how he was trained by Barnabas for ministry, who was in turn trained by the twelve apostles. So it makes sense that he would build his ministry on a similar foundation of small home based fellowships.

Speaking years later to the elders at Ephesus, Paul reminded them how he had taught them publicly, and "from house to house" (Acts 20:20). This was a special farewell address to this church, and it's clear Paul was encouraging them to remember his model of ministry, so they could continue it.

And Paul's writings are similarly filled with counsel for believers to encourage, support, and nurture one another. In fact, the "one another" verses seem endless. And Paul urged them specifically to press together in love and unity (I Thessalonians

3:12, I Corinthians 1:10), and model these things to the world. Paul knew this was the secret to the tremendous growth of the New Testament church—and that so long as they continued to use the keys Jesus had given, the church would prosper and thrive.

While we don't have time to exhaust the subject here, it's clear homes continued to be centers of evangelism all through the inspired record. We read, for example, of groups meeting in the homes of Narcissus, Stephanus, Aquila and Priscilla, Jason, Philemon, Onesiphorus, Gaius, Lydia, Jason, Justus and Crispus, and Philip to name just a few. Home based fellowship were everywhere.

You can certainly find examples of public speakers, like Peter and Paul. And you can find examples of personal Bible work, like Philip and the Ethiopian, or Jesus and the two men on the road to Emmaus. But overwhelmingly, for the average member—ministry was centered in homes, and powered by love and unity. And that essentially is the definition of a Care Group.

Care Groups are powerful because they provide a warm and supportive environment for both believers and unbelievers to grow spiritually. They give participants a place they can belong--in a world that is increasingly fragmented and alienated. Care Groups minister to the whole person: their mental, social, physical, and spiritual needs. And they give seekers time to build relationships with other believers as they work through spiritual issues.

And today, just as then, searching hearts will be drawn to such a group.

I am convinced, that if we examine the evidence objectively, the conclusion is clear. The early church reached a world by opening their homes for ministry. It may be an adjustment to get back to this model today, as our homes have become fortress sanctuaries, in which we barricade ourselves away from the world. But if we are seriously about not just finishing the work, but doing it the way Jesus taught, we are going to want to get back to this model of ministry.

Your next question may be, is this really going to work today? Let's explore that in the next section.

# Clear Instructions
## Study Questions

How would you summarize the various instructions Jesus gave to His disciples about how to do ministry?

How would you describe the methods the apostles used at Pentecost? What were the results?

What method did Paul use in his ministries? How are his epistles filled with instructions about how to relate one another as believers?

Explain what makes a Care Group so effective at drawing people to Christ:

Additional Notes:

# Overcoming Obstacles
## Chapter 4

So far we've looked at Care Groups as a powerful model for ministry, primarily because it can enable the average member to become effective in soul-winning. We've also looked at what makes it such an effective model, compared to other more typical approaches—like public evangelism and Bible work. And how it avoids many of the problems associated with them.

We've also looked at the biblical evidence for making small, home-based fellowships the foundation of our evangelistic efforts. How the New Testament church prospered because it zeroed in on homes, encouraging every member to open their homes, and use the keys of love and unity to win their family, friends and neighbors. It certainly worked for them.

But just because something can work, doesn't mean it will work. In fact, you may have even tried small groups of one sort or another in the past with lackluster results. You may have even tried implementing the Care Group model explicitly, and not seen the results you hoped for. And you may be wondering why it didn't work.

I've studied this question carefully, and have come to the conclusion there are two main problems that will keep your Care Group program from succeeding. And then I'm going to suggest a somewhat simple fix.

**Problem #1: Busy Churches**

In my experience, most churches are structured in a way that makes it extremely difficult to get Care Groups going. Basically, even small churches attempt to operate a rather massive church program, and it takes every person giving all they can to keep that edifice running. If you've ever served on a nominating committee trying to fill all those church offices, you know how challenging it is to keep every slot filled.

In other words, churches are busy. And your most committed leaders are probably already wearing three or four hats, or more. With so many programs going there's hardly any room to add something new. And even if you can get a Care Group or two going, there's a good chance they are going to remain tangential, off to the side, peripheral. Such Care Groups are unlikely to ever become a core part of the culture of your congregation, and will instead remain just one small ministry squeezed in among many.

What we really want is to make Care Groups the foundation of our outreach efforts. To get our best leaders involved leading teams, and a majority of our members plugged in as participants. Something powerful happens when most of your members start getting serious about winning souls—and start seeing results. But it's something you are unlikely to experience so long as most of your members are busy running programs. The shift in focus from programs to people is like flipping a switch.

This was something I didn't really notice about Gateway my first time there. Other than organizing the weekly lesson study period and a worship service, their churches ran almost no other ministries. Actually, they ran all sorts of ministries—but they were all done through their Care Groups, as I'll explain in a moment.

Bottom line: it's a hard ask for someone already saddled by constant programs, committees, and events to give one night a week to a Care Group. Without a major transformation in how our churches are structured, you are unlikely to experience Care Group ministry success.

## Problem #2: Cuckoo Clock Care Groups

The second problem is related, but more on the Care Group side. Because we're so used to running programs as a church, it's easy to fall into the habit of running our Care Groups just like any other church program.

I sometimes refer to this as the cuckoo clock syndrome. That is, we go our way through the week, without any real engagement with the other members of our Care Group, and then pop out of our cuckoo clock for an hour or two at the appointed hour, whenever our Care Group meeting time rolls around. Then once that meeting is over, we retreat back into our individual lives once again, until the next meeting.

A Care Group run like this is not going to work. Care Groups are supposed to be a manifestation of true Christian community. A demonstration of the twin principles of love and unity. It's all about building real relationships, with fellow believers, and then letting that fellowship spill over to the seekers who become part of these groups.

Members of the Care Groups I studied at Gateway were real friends, in regular communication with each other. Core members would meet together weekly outside of Care Group to plan and assess their progress, and pray for each meeting. And they would get together socially at other times, inviting seekers to participate in those events too. Care Groups were more like a family.

Perhaps more important: each Care Group was a hub for ministry. That is, ministry didn't need to be done by the church, because it was being done in the Care Groups. They would run health programs, do literature distribution, operate Bible schools, and any other kind of outreach you might see in a local church—but these efforts were all operated by the various Care Groups. And as a result, there was a steady flow of new seekers into each group. In fact, this was a definite expectation—if you don't have seekers, it isn't a Care Group.

Now you can sometimes get a Care Group started, and wrangle a seeker or two to come out. But if your group is not doing some sort of outreach together, those seekers will eventually either get baptized or stop coming. And you will soon find yourself looking around a living room filled with nothing but church members. A Care Group like this is doomed to fail. For there is no way to win souls, if there aren't any around to win.

## A Simple Solution

Both these problems are serious, and at first glance may seem insurmountable. Our program focus, as opposed to a relationship focus, is so pervasive it is difficult to imagine either churches or Care Groups ever being very fruitful. But there is an obvious solution.

Think about it this way: our churches are typically ministry rich, but have little follow-up or nurture in place for the people they reach—leading to negligible results. Care Groups, on the other hand, do a great job supporting and growing people, but they are typically ministry deficient, and as a result starved for seekers.

The obvious solution is to link them together.

There are several ways to do this. If you are starting a new church, like Gateway, you can be intentional about this from the start. You can expect every member to plug into some Care Group, and funnel all ministry through those teams. But if you are part of an established church, I can assure you, it will be difficult to make that change.

Another option is to have local church ministries start their own Care Groups, or to have Care Groups start their own ministries. But if you have both already, there's an even easier shortcut: you can have ministries and Care Groups adopt each other. I especially like this option, because it is probably the quickest way to revitalize both.

When I was a pastor, our church suffered from the exact problems described above. We had a busy church running all sorts of ministries. And we ran multiple Care Groups. But none of them were linked together, and neither were very effective as a result. In hindsight, I can see now that there were plenty of ways to fix that. For example:

One of our ministries was a foodbank. That ministry was doing a great job attracting large numbers of seekers and distributing food to needy families. But not one participant ever joined our church. We could have easily had one of our Care Groups partner with that ministry—to work closely with it, and find ways to funnel interested people into a Care Group.

We had a monthly cooking school that was pretty good at attracting seekers interested in learning healthful recipes. We could have easily linked a Care Group with that ministry, and invited participants to join a Care Group, emphasizing a free weekly vegetarian meal.

We ran vibrant Adventurers and Pathfinder programs, and some of these kids were non-members. We could have easily linked in a Care Group focused on families, perhaps covering parenting topics. In fact, theoretically, we might have even been able to run that in parallel with those ministries.

And there are many more possibilities. You could start a Care Group for families in your church school. Women that come to your women's ministry events. Your youth group. A group for seniors. Participants in your Bible school. People that come out to your clothes distribution center. The reality is a Care Group can be attached to pretty much any ministry, and when that happens, both will be dramatically strengthened.

If there are no viable ministries in your church—your Care Group will just need to start one.

## A Gardening Lesson

If you've ever grown a garden, you know there are three main steps: sow the seed, cultivate the plants, and finally, reap the harvest. I love the sowing and reaping stages. Seeing all those neat little pristine rows with tiny seedlings popping up. Or coming back later and harvesting huge baskets of produce. And churches typically love doing these kinds of ministries too.

Seminars, concerts, door to door surveying, literature distribution, community service projects, etc. All of these are sowing events—where we make initial contact with someone in our community. It's exciting because we get to meet new people. Systematic Bible instruction and public evangelistic meetings are our more common reaping activities. These are exciting too, because we get to see the culmination of a person's journey to faith.

The real work of gardening, however, is the cultivation stage in between. The constant weeding, fertilizing, watering, mulching, and fighting pests, and so on, required to keep our plants healthy and strong. But this is where the real growth takes place. And as any good gardener will tell you, you can't just plant seeds in the spring and come back in the fall for a harvest. It simply doesn't work that way.

But that's often exactly what we do in our churches. Isn't it?

A Care Group is the ideal environment to cultivate that all important growth. Those we meet through our various outreach ministries, can be invited to join a friendly group, for a meal and simple study in someone's home. Over time they build friendships, get answers to questions, and begin to see God work in their life. And gradually, they start taking small steps toward Christ. This growth takes place naturally, it isn't rushed, or pressured. Given enough time, a person in that kind of environment almost inevitably starts moving toward faith.

A Care Group bridges the gap between first contact and conversion. Between sowing and reaping. Without the long hard work of cultivation—caring for your plants through those long summer days—few gardens will produce, no matter how much you sow or how hard you try and reap. Similarly, it is the long, hard work of caring for people between first contact and final conversion that ensures consistent soul winning success.

If we are serious about wanting to see our churches become soul winning successes, we need to think seriously about structural transformation. Of building a different foundation for our outreach efforts. Of linking Care Groups and local church ministries together. And more importantly, of reorganizing our ministry around the love and unity that can best be cultivated in small groups.

## Overcoming Obstacles
### Study Questions

What is the first common obstacle to successful Care Groups? How does it hinder Care Group success?

What is the second obstacle to successful Care Groups? How does it hinder Care Group success?

Explain the simple method you can use to help solve both of these problems. Give some examples of how this could work:

What are the three main steps in growing a garden? What does each step correspond to in terms of church ministry?

How important are Care Groups in this process? What happens when there is no cultivation in a garden?


Additional Notes:

# The Need to Lead
## Chapter 5

In our last section we looked at two major obstacles to successful Care Groups. Churches that are too busy running programs. And Care Groups that don't have a steady stream of new seekers. Fortunately, the solution for these problems is not all that difficult. It simply involves linking ministries and Care Groups together.

But there's another big obstacle to running an effective Care Group ministry, and in some ways, this is an even more challenging problem, because it will require significantly more effort to overcome it.

And I'm talking about the need for leadership.

The bottom line is this: the success and failure of your Care Groups will be largely correlated to the skill of your team leaders. And ultimately, the growth of your Care Group ministry (how many teams you have) is going to be constrained by the number of trained leaders available. And good training takes time. So for your efforts to thrive and grow, you are going to want to start thinking about developing future leaders right now.

Let's talk a bit about why leadership is so important...

## Ministry Skills

So far in this class, we've looked primarily at why Care Groups are so important. Why they are so foundational to effective outreach. But we haven't talked about the mechanics of how to run a Care Group. To implement a true Care Group, there's actually a fair bit to learn:

- When to meet, and where
- The typical weekly program
- The proper use of food
- How to cultivate community
- How to do the icebreaker
- Ideal Bible study topics
- How to make the Bible study interactive
- Dealing with questions/objections
- Connecting with seekers
- Managing the sharing time
- Keys to praying together
- Calling for decisions
- Nurturing faith and discipleship
- Leadership roles and responsibilities
- The replication process
- Organizing multiple teams
- Church relations and support
- And much more...

In other words, a Care Group is not just some randomly thrown together small group, but rather a highly specific approach to using home-based fellowships for evangelism. And if you want to be as effective as possible in your Care Group ministry, it's important that your teams understand this model and follow it closely.

One reason this is so important, is so your team can function as unitedly as possible. Remember that unity is one of the twin keys to evangelistic success. When members in your group are divided about how to do certain things, you introduce the potential for conflict and division. And you minimize that vital key.

Perhaps more important, this model has been hammered out through years of frontline ministry with real live seekers, with plenty of tinkering and tweaking to figure out what works best. And specifically, what best communicates love to the seekers in our group. What creates a feeling of belonging. Of friendship. What will convince them your group truly cares. That's the other key to success.

Fortunately, these skills can be learned fairly easily. Our own ministry has developed a nine week training program called Team Tactics that goes over exactly how to launch, lead, and unleash a Care Group, developed in close cooperation with leaders at Gateway. It's the perfect way to learn and practice your Care Groups skills when first getting your team started. We highly recommend it.

The reality is, many churches have long lost the ability to really interact with and engage unbelievers, and the approaches we typically use have become increasingly ineffective. If we want to start seeing better results, we need to learn new methods of modeling love and unity to those we are trying to reach. That means your Care Group leaders need to be well trained.

**Real Discipleship**

There's another reason training is so important, and it's this: soul winning is hard work, and it's going to require team members who are spiritually mature. As important as the mechanics of running a Care Group can be—the basics of personal discipleship is even more important.

When the core members are spending regular time studying, memorizing, and applying the Word of God, that will spill out in their daily life. And in the Care Group meetings. They can model the process of truly internalizing and assimilating Scripture. And they can answer questions in a more meaningful, Bible-based way. The better your core members exemplify a Bible-centered life, the more your seekers will be drawn to explore the Word too.

Another critical area is prayer. Core members who spend real time in prayer, both individually, and together as a group, claiming specific promises for the seekers in their Care Group—and do this consistently—are going to see different results than teams where this doesn't happen. Even more, learning to pray comfortably with seekers, who then see those prayers answered can be life-changing for that person just getting to know God. Effective prayer is vital.

A third spoke of discipleship is personal obedience. This includes things like prioritization and time management. Core members who are truly committed to, and willing to sacrifice for, the Great Commission will participate in team meetings faithfully. When that is lacking, attendance can fluctuate, or worse, fizzle. Seekers also need to see believers wrestling to live by Biblical principles, and gaining victories. Or occasionally stumble, and then recover themselves. All this can be modeled firsthand in a Care Group.

And last but not least, every core member should be armed with good witnessing skills. To know how to talk with seekers in a friendly, engaging way. To be able to share their personal testimony clearly and compellingly. To have a firm grasp on the Gospel, and be able to point seekers to heaven's power in real, concrete ways. And ultimately, to lead that seeker to give their heart to Jesus at the appropriate time. If our lives are fully centered in Christ, we will invariably lift Christ up, and seekers will be drawn in.

**The Next Generation**

This list is not exhaustive of course, but rather just illustrates my point. The stronger the personal discipleship of your core members, the more effective your Care Group will be at winning souls. Care Group ministry is not a mechanical work, it is a spiritual work. And we need to have the Holy Spirit flooding through our Care Groups. That means our leaders must be spiritual.

In addition to the specialized Team Tactics program mentioned above, FAST also has a comprehensive discipleship curriculum that has helped thousands grow in their walk with Christ. It consists of three separate study courses, and takes approximately nine months to complete. The first course, Survival Kit, is a five week introduction to Bible memorization, and the fundamentals of the Christian life. Basic Training is next, with nine weeks of practical instructions in key areas of discipleship—including each of the areas listed above. And finally, Revival Keys wraps things up, by encouraging believers to band together in Spirit-filled ministry teams. Teams that can become the heart of future Care Groups. You can learn more about how to use these resources by reading our free Leaders Manual at *http://fast.st/lm*.

Though it goes beyond the scope of this class, we strongly recommend every member of your core team go through this training track as a core part of their preparation for Care Group leadership. And that you begin a FAST training class in your church as quickly as possible, to start training the next generation of leaders. For if you don't, the time may well come when your groups are filled to bursting and ready to replicate—but you won't have anyone qualified to lead that new group.

Keeping this training cycle running is the key to multiplying your care groups. Running one successful group will never transform your church. The goal is to run an ever expanding number of teams. And that means planning ahead to train the next generation of leadership.

There's much more to say on this topic, but in my view, the key characteristic of leadership is vision. Once we are gripped by a fervent determination to multiply spiritually, our primary goal will be to see every member become a worker. To see every member learn to reproduce. And Care Groups will be at the heart of that vision.

# The Need to Lead
Study Questions

Explain how a lack of leadership can constrain the growth of your Care Group ministry:

Why is it important that your Care Group leaders understand the mechanics of running a successful Care Group?

List some of the critical skills your team needs to learn?

Why is solid discipleship training so essential to effective Care Group ministry? What kinds of subjects does this need to include?

What plan should you have in place to ensure you are preparing the next generation of leaders for your growing Care Group ministry.

Additional Notes:

# How to Get Started
## Chapter 6

The explosive growth of the New Testament church was built on an engine of small, home-based fellowships that gathered regularly for a meal, Bible study, sharing, and prayer. Where group members could invite friends to an environment that models love and unity. That supported spiritual growth. And there, hearts were touched by the transforming power of the Holy Spirit. The same engine will yield similar results today.

We call this kind of approach to evangelism: Care Groups.

By now you may be already thinking about how to start a Care Group of your own. The next few paragraphs will guide you through a few simple steps to get your team going. It is not especially difficult, which is one of the great advantages of Care Group ministry—pretty much anyone can do it. But it will take some planning, preparation, and prayer. Follow these suggestions closely, and your Care Group will soon be up and running!

**Build A Nucleus**

Every Care Group starts with a call to leadership. If you sense that God is calling you to help launch and lead a new team, your first task is going to be much prayer for God's blessing in the formation of your team. It's not an easy process, and His leading is going to be essential.

Pray specifically that God would lead you to just the right assistant (or two) willing to join you in this adventure. And then together, to prayerfully gather a few people more to round out your core team. A good healthy Care Group should include a minimum of 4-6 members from at least three families.

Look for people you work well with, and who share your burden for ministry. If you are not sure who to ask, consider giving potential partners a copy of this book—and ask them to read it and let you know what they think. Those who grasp the strategies and principles of a Care Group, and are excited about it, will make your best partners. It will also help ensure everyone is united on how the team runs.

*Note: If you are working through our full discipleship training program, the most obvious way to start a team is for your existing class to become the core team for a new Care Group. Simply select a leader, assistant, and core members, from among your class and continue the planning process from there.*

## Master the Mechanics

The next step is to start meeting together as a group and begin developing your Care Group skills. As noted in our last section, our Team Tactics program is a nine week training program designed to help you master the mechanics of this approach to ministry.

We recommend running this class as a practice Care Group. That is, choose one evening a week to meet. Begin with a meal, and time of fellowship. Do the Bible study together, end with a time of sharing and prayer—just as if you were in a regular Care Group. The goal is not to invite seekers at this point, but for your group to begin to grow together, as friends. To get a feel for what a Care Group is like. And to acquire the skills needed to run one successfully. These nine weeks also give you a chance to plan out all the details for your launch.

Throughout this entire process, you will want to continue in fervent prayer for your growing team, that God would give each team member a burden for souls, and a commitment to working together toward that. Pray God will give your team the love and unity it will need to be effective. Without prayer, even the best skills will be insufficient.

**Plan the Launch**

There are a number of details you will need to settle during this preparation process, before the official launch of your Care Group. Here are just some of the things you will want to consider in your planning. Once again, remember to be prayerful at each step in the process:

- Location. Where will you meet? It is better to use a home than a church, and to maintain a consistent location rather than rotating from week to week. To help distribute responsibilities more evenly, we recommend choosing someone other than the leader or assistant to serve as the host.
- Times and Dates. Which night of the week, and at what time will you meet? For how long? Different times may work better for different groups, including daytime meetings, which may work better for stay-at-home moms or retirees who don't like to drive at night.
- Responsibilities. Divide up group tasks among the team. Who will lead out in the Bible study? The sharing time? The prayer? How will meals be

arranged? If duties are rotated, what will be the schedule? Make sure everyone has a job: helping with transportation, sending birthday cards, doing announcements each week, etc. All can help!

■ Study Topic. Settle on a topic for your first study series. Choose something relevant, interesting, popular to help attract people. Pass out fliers in the neighborhood where your team will meet, put up fliers, and post announcements on social media. Be creative in promoting it!

■ A Prayer List. Encourage each team member to suggest a few names of people they would like to see come—and begin praying for them as a group. When your launch date arrives, urge each member to invite those people to come. Some people may need to be invited multiple times before they decide to visit.

■ Ministry Partnerships. If possible, connect with some ministry to promote your Care Group. If there is no existing church ministry with access to seekers, you will need to launch some new ministry to generate your own stream of contacts. Care Groups without an active "fishing pond" may find it difficult to attract new members.

■ Church Promotion. Actively promote your new team in your local church. Seek out and give personal invitations to newly baptized members, struggling members, non-attending members, visitors and guests, attending non-members, etc. Ask regular members who know people that might benefit from your group, to invite them. Or better still, to bring them.

- Communication. Throughout the whole process, work closely with your pastor and church leaders—keeping them informed of your plans. Care Groups work best when well integrated into the overall evangelistic vision of a local church. Counsel with them on how best to do that.

Once everything is sketched out, it will be time to put your plans into action. Set a start date, get busy inviting, and launch! Don't be discouraged if your team is small at first. It just takes one seeker to start.

**Keep it Going**

To ensure your Care Group launch gets off to a strong, healthy start it's important to press together. Here are a few thoughts on how to do this.

First, find ways to do life together as a group outside your weekly meetings. As noted earlier, we must resist the temptation to see Care Group as just another event on your calendar. The goal is real relationships, and that's hard to do just once a week. Schedule occasional outings for the whole group: maybe a picnic at the park, a hike on some trail, or a trip to the zoo. If your church has some special event like a cooking school, lecture, or music concert, make it a group event and drag everyone along you can. Look for community service opportunities: raking leaves, feeding the homeless, volunteering for some charity. These kinds of activities create great memories and will bind your team together more tightly.

Second, encourage individual relationships between seekers and members within the group. Exchange phone numbers and emails. Connect on social media. Then use these channels: share a promise, comment on a social media post, give someone a call, send a post card from your exotic vacation location. Acknowledge birthdays, anniversaries, and important holidays. Check up on individuals going through difficult times, and maybe grab a lunch together. Often these interactions outside your meetings will prove key to the success you experience inside your meetings.

And third, it's good to have periodic meetings with your core team, separate from the rest of the larger group. Use these times to evaluate and assess how things are going—and devise ways to tweak and improve results going forward. And especially, to pray. Try to meet at least once a week for this (by phone or video), to pray for specific seekers, and for the success of your team in general. Get together in person every once in awhile—to give core members a chance to fellowship among themselves, and celebrate the successes of your team. As your ministry grows, these times will become increasingly special to your team.

So there you have it: simple tips on how to get your team up and running. Build a nucleus, master the mechanics, plan your launch, and then keep your team going. Stick with this plan, and your team will be sure to get off to a great start! And bathe every step in prayer. You will soon have many wonderful memories, decisions, and friendships, to look back on. And almost certainly, baptisms. It will happen!!!

One more section to go, where we look at our final key...

# How to Get Started
## Study Questions

What is the basic process for building a nucleus of leaders and core members for your Care Group?

What is the recommended approach for equipping your team with the essential skills of running a Care Group?

Make a list of some of the details you will need to plan out when preparing your launch?

What are some things you can do to help ensure your Care Group continues on in a healthy way?

Explain the importance of living life together?

Additional Notes:

# Fellowship of the Church
Chapter 7

Before ending our brief study together, allow me to challenge your thinking for just a moment more. In particular, I want to talk about what the word "church" really means. Though it's often used today to refer to the actual building where we worship God, most of us know the real church is the people, not the building. You and me, we make up the church. Not the studs and drywall.

But I believe this topic merits going a bit deeper. And it relates to this topic of Care Groups directly.

**The Ekklesia**

The Greek word translated "church" in the New Testament is the word "ekklesia", and it means a gathering or assembly. So when God's people come out for worship each week at the local church building, that gathering or assembly is the church.

But that is not the only time God's people gather together, right?

Suppose you have a large conference, or campmeeting, where believers from many different local churches gather together. That's the church too, isn't it? And what about something even larger? Like a national convention, or even a large global general conference. That's the church too.

But it can take smaller forms as well. In the New Testament, churches frequently met in homes, as we've seen. This was partly because they did not often have other large meeting locations, but that's beside the point. Clearly, even a small group meeting together in a home, is a gathering, or assembly. It's church.

If you've ever sat on some church committee or board, that was a church meeting too. In fact, Jesus made it clear, this principle extends to the smallest level possible. "For where two or three are gathered together in my name, there am I in the midst of them" (Matthew 18:20). Even two believers who gather or assemble in the name of Christ—form a church.

This is not to say, there is no purpose for a local church. There is. Just like there's a place for conferences, unions, and divisions. And a place for small boards and committees. They all serve important purposes in keeping the body of Christ structured and organized. My point is simply that the essence of church is not structure, but fellowship. It's about believers coming together in Christ.

## Koinonia

Which brings us to another Greek word: koinonia. This word is most often translated in the New Testament as fellowship or communion, and refers to sharing or participating in something together. It describes both our fellowship with Christ, and our fellowship with one another as believers.

Paul understood the heart of his ministry to be centered on inviting others into our fellowship as believers. To join us as we gather or assemble together. In one of his most profound descriptions of his life work, Paul wrote this:

*Ephesians 3:7,9*
*I was made a minister according to the gift of*
*the grace of God given unto me by the*
*effectual working of his power ... to make all*
*men see what is the fellowship of the mystery,*
*which from the beginning of the world hath*
*been hid in God.*

That mystery of course, was that we could "be strengthened with might by his Spirit in the inner man; that Christ may dwell in your hearts by faith" (Ephesians 3:16-17). Every person who shares in or participates in this mystery through the Gospel is a part of that fellowship. And Paul's longing was for all men to experience that fellowship for themselves. To taste the life of faith.

He went on to explain the key to inviting others into this fellowship. Namely, that WE be "rooted and grounded in love" (Ephesians 3:17). That WE be able to comprehend "with all saints what is the breadth, and length, and depth, and height" of the "love of Christ" (Ephesians 3:18-19). That WE might be "filled with all the fulness of God" (Ephesians 3:19). In other words, the way to invite others into our fellowship, is to enter into fellowship with Christ more fully ourselves. It would be through the twin keys of love and unity.

And the end result of this process? There would be glory to God "in the church by Christ Jesus throughout all ages, world without end" (Ephesians 3:21). That is, God is glorified by how believers interact with each other. This in fact, is "the eternal purpose which he purposed in Christ Jesus our Lord", that the "manifold wisdom of God" would be made known to the "principalities and powers in heavenly places ... by the church" (Ephesians 3:10-11). It's not revealed primarily by individuals, but by groups—in how they relate to one another.

The point here seems clear: God's ultimate purpose is to reveal His character through the fellowship enjoyed by His church. And the heart of evangelism is simply calling friends and family to join in that fellowship. Something so sweet, it has an almost irresistible drawing power.

Thinking about ministry in this way, only highlights the need for Care Groups. Their importance to the whole great controversy between good and evil. And how important they are to our own life of faith.

## Will it Really Work?

So I've made my case for Care Groups. Maybe you are still wondering if Care Groups can really work today. Maybe things are just too different in our day, and this approach is longer effective. Is it really worth making the effort to learn a whole new approach to ministry? Can we really expect the average believer to win souls through Care Groups?

Allow me to change that question around. Is there anything else that can?

I shared when first starting this course, that I spent a good part of my life as an itinerant preacher, traveling to endless churches. And in all those churches, I can't think of one where the average member was regularly and consistently being equipped to win souls to Christ. That is, until I encountered Gateway. Or to put it differently, it's not just that Care Groups have the potential to work, it's the only thing I've ever seen that does work.

This is not to say that there aren't other growing churches. Some may have an exceptional pastor, who is a powerful speaker. Maybe a church has specially strong vision and leadership. Maybe there's a large infusion of financial resources. Or a significant amount of transfer growth. These churches are rare as well, to be sure—but they exist. But I've never seen one of these churches grow because the average member is being equipped to start winning souls within just a couple years of joining that church. And if we are serious about spiritual multiplication, that has to be our goal.

But at a more fundamental level, Care Groups are key because they are a fulfillment of God's eternal purpose for the church. That believers could gather together in homes around the world, and enjoy powerful fellowship together. A fellowship marked by the twin keys of love and unity. A fellowship where every member is truly cared for, and feels a true sense of belonging.

Which means evangelism is essentially inviting others into our fellowship, so unbelievers can see the character of Christ lived out in the lives of His people. So Christ can be lifted up through our interactions. By how we care for each other. Personally, I don't think anything else has more drawing power to win souls to the kingdom.

And ultimately, this kind of fellowship is the solution to an even larger problem. The enemy has slandered the character of God. Intelligent beings from throughout the whole universe are looking down. And in particular, they are watching to see how believers interact when they gather together. Unbelievably, God's plan is to resolve the whole Great Controversy by showing to the entire universe, His character, revealed through true Christian fellowship. And there's no better place to present that evidence, than a Care Group.

We see some of this in large gatherings of believers, like conferences and campmeetings. And we can see it at times in our formal weekly worship services. But the best place to reveal the love of Christ, is in our homes, with family and friends—where we live out and share life together.

And that's what a Care Group is all about: CARE stands for Christ's Attitude Reflected in Everybody. And that's what it's all about.

# Fellowship of the Church
## Study Questions

Define the real meaning of the Greek word "Ekklesia"? What does it suggest about Care Groups?

What does the Greek word "Koinonia" mean? What does it suggest about Care Groups?

Explain the importance of the twin keys of love and unity, and especially, their role in resolving the Great Controversy.

Why are Care Groups such a central part of God's plan to reveal His character to the world?

What does the acronym CARE stand for?

Additional Notes:

# FAST Missions
Cutting-Edge Tools and Training

Ready to become a Revival Agent? FAST Missions can help! Our comprehensive training curriculum will give you the skills you need to take in God's Word effectively, live it out practically, and pass it on to others consistently.

Eager to start memorizing God's Word? Our powerful keys will transform your ability to hide Scripture in your heart.

Want to explore the secrets of "real life" discipleship? Our next level training zooms in on critical keys to growth, like Bible study, prayer, time management, and more.

Want to become a worker in the cause of Christ? Our most advanced training is designed to give you the exact ministry skills you need to see revival spread.

For more information, please visit us at:
**WWW.FASTMISSIONS.COM**

# Study Guides

Looking for life-changing study guides to use in your small group or Bible study class? These resources have been used by thousands around the world. You could be next!

### Survival Kit

Want to learn how to memorize Scripture effectively? These study guides will teach you 10 keys to memorization, all drawn straight from the Bible. Our most popular course ever!

### Basic Training

Discover nuts and bolts keys to the core skills of discipleship: prayer, Bible study, time management, and more. Then learn how to share these skills with others. It is the course that launched our ministry!

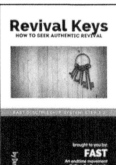

### Revival Keys

Now as never before, God's people need revival. And these guides can show you how to spark revival in your family, church, and community. A great revival is coming. Are you ready?

# Online Classes

Want to try out some of the resources available at FAST? Here is just a small sampling of courses from among dozens of personal and small group study resources:

### Crash Course
Discover Bible-based keys to effective memorization.
*http://fast.st/cc*

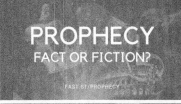

### Fact or Fiction
Does the Bible really predict future events? You be the judge.
*http://fast.st/prophecy*

### Monkey Business
Find out how evolution flunks the science test.
*http://fast.st/monkey*

### Revive
Want more of God's Spirit? Learn how to pursue revival.
*http://fast.st/revive*

### The Lost Art
Rediscover New Testament keys to making disciples.
*http://fast.st/lostart*

# Digital Tools

FAST offers a number of powerful "apps for the soul" you can use to grow in your walk with God. And many of these are completely free to anyone with an account. Some of these include:

### Review Engine
Our powerful review engine is designed to help ensure effective longterm Bible memorization. Give it a try, it works!

### Bible Reading
An innovative Bible reading tool to help you read through the entire Bible, at your own pace, and in any order you want.

### Prayer Journal
Use this tool to organize important requests, and we'll remind you to pray for them on the schedule you want.

### Time Management
Learn how to be more productive, by keeping track of what you need to do and when. Just log in daily and get stuff done.

For more information about more than twenty tools like these, please visit us at *http://fast.st/tools*.

# Books

If the content of this little book stirred your heart, look for these titles by the same author.

### For Such A Time...
A challenging look at the importance of memorization for the last days, including topics such as the Three Angel's messages and the Latter Rain.

### Moral Machinery
Discover how our spiritual, mental, and physical faculties work together using the sanctuary as a blueprint. Astonishing insights that could revolutionize your life!

### The Movement
Discover God's plan to finish the work through a powerful endtime movement. Gain critical insights into what lies just ahead for the remnant!

Printed in Great Britain
by Amazon

32888409R00040